<u>INDEX</u>

The Clinton Foundation

The Clinton Foundation is a nonprofit organization founded in 2001 by former President Bill Clinton. It seeks to bring people together using money to find creative solutions to global challenges. In 2005, the foundation established the Clinton Global Initiative in order to "convene global leaders to create and implement innovative solutions to the world's most pressing challenges." Hillary Clinton joined in 2013 after leaving the State Department. Since its founding, the foundation has raised nearly $2 billion.

Hillary Clinton is running for president, but due to her advanced age, inability to think on her feet, and unquenchable lust for money, she would like to avoid having to actually campaign for as long as possible. For the most part, the national press has seemed content to let her get away with this.

However, a few enterprising reporters are attempting to legitimately vet the presumed Democratic nominee, and have begun to investigate the inner workings of the Clinton Foundation. In doing so, they've uncovered some troubling facts.

The string of revelations began when the Wall Street Journal **reported** that the Clinton Foundation had quietly lifted its ban on accepting donations from foreign governments. The ban was put in place at the request of the Obama Administration in 2009, when Hillary Clinton started her tenure as Secretary of State. Soon after she quit her job in 2013, however, the foundation began accepting millions of dollars from foreign government donors, including Saudi Arabia, Oman, and the United Arab Emirates.

The *Washington Post* **reported** that the Clinton Foundation accepted millions of dollars in foreign government donations while Hillary was serving in the State Department. Most of those donations were technically allowed due to the many exemptions included in the so-called "ban." However, at least one of those donations—$500,000 from the Algerian government—violated the ban, and was not reported to the State Department's ethics office.

The Clinton Foundation takes money from just about everyone, including many of the giant corporations liberals claim to despise, such as ExxonMobil, Citigroup, Barclays, Pfizer, Goldman Sachs, Morgan Stanley, Bank of America, General Electric, Monsanto, McDonald's, Walmart, among many others. The *Washington Post* **noted** that many of the foundation's biggest donors are foreign citizens who are unable to give money directly to U.S. political campaigns.

The Clintons have attended a number of events with foundation donor Victor Pinchuk, a Ukrainian steel magnate who has been **accused** of unfair trade practices. Frank Guistra is a Canadian mining tycoon and member of the

Clintons' inner circle who has donated tens of millions of dollars to the foundation. In 2005, Bill Clinton accompanied Guistra on a trip to Kazakhstan for a meeting with the country's strongman president. After the meeting, Guistra's company was awarded some lucrative mining contracts in Kazakhstan, and Guistra donated more than $30 million to the Clinton Foundation. Both men deny accusations of a quid pro quo.

During her time as Secretary of State, Hillary Clinton helped secure lucrative foreign contracts for companies who had donated millions to the Clinton Foundation, including General Electric, ExxonMobil, Microsoft, and Boeing. In addition to the donations, these companies spent millions lobbying the State Department during Clinton's tenure.

The *New York Times* politely urged the Clinton Foundation to sever its ties to foreign governments, but others weren't so kind. *National Journal*'s Ron Fournier denounced the foundation's decision as "sleazy" and a "clear conflict of interest." *Bloomberg*'s John Heileman called it "totally insane." Even*Salon* described the situation as a "ridiculous" "mess."

Soon after the 10th anniversary of the foundation bearing his name, Bill Clinton met with a small group of aides and two lawyers from Simpson Thacher& Bartlett. Two weeks of interviews with Clinton Foundation executives and former employees had led the lawyers to some unsettling conclusions.

The review echoed criticism of Mr. Clinton's early years in the White House: For all of its successes, the Clinton Foundation had become a sprawling concern, supervised by a rotating board of old Clinton hands, vulnerable to distraction and threatened by conflicts of interest. It ran multimillion-dollar deficits for several years, despite vast amounts of money flowing in.

And concern was rising inside and outside the organization about Douglas J. Band, a onetime personal assistant to Mr. Clinton who had started a lucrative corporate consulting firm — which Mr. Clinton joined as a paid adviser — while overseeing the Clinton Global Initiative, the foundation's glitzy annual gathering of chief executives, heads of state, and celebrities.

As reported by the International Business Times, while serving as secretary of state, Clinton was lobbied by human rights groups and union leaders to address the Colombian government's abuse of striking oil workers, some of whom had been threatened at gunpoint by the military. Meanwhile, the oil company in question, Pacific Rubiales, was promising millions to the Clinton Foundation.

Hillary's State Department wound up publicly hailing Colombia's commitment to human rights reform — and that statement allowed the United States to continue funding the Colombian military.Today, the founder of Pacific Rubiales is a board member of the Clinton Foundation.

And as *Politico* reported, a major phosphate company owned by the Moroccan government has just pledged at least $1 million to the foundation. In 2011, Clinton's State Department assailed Morocco as a corrupt state guilty of "arbitrary arrests and corruption in all branches of government." Women in Morocco are still subjugated by Islamic rule, yet last September, Hillary Clinton's public stance on the government had changed.

The Clinton Foundation, which has 350 employees in 180 countries, remains largely powered by Mr. Clinton's global celebrity and his ability to connect corporate executives, A-listers and government officials.

For most of the foundation's existence, its leadership has been dominated by loyal veterans of the Clintons' political lives. Ira C. Magaziner, who was a Rhodes scholar with Mr. Clinton and ran Mrs. Clinton's failed attempt at a health care overhaul in the 1990s, is widely credited as the driving force behind the foundation's largest project, the Clinton Health Access Initiative, which, among other efforts, negotiates bulk purchasing agreements and price discounts on lifesaving medicines.

Mr. Band, who arrived at the White House in 1995 and worked his way up to become Mr. Clinton's closest personal aide, standing behind the president on golf courses and the global stage, helped build the foundation's fund-raising structure. He conceived of and for many years helped run the Clinton Global Initiative, the annual conference that draws hundreds of business leaders and heads of state to New York City where attendees are pushed to make specific philanthropic commitments.

Today, big-name companies vie to buy sponsorships at prices of $250,000 and up, money that has helped subsidize the foundation's annual operating costs. Last year, the foundation and two subsidiaries had revenues of more than $214 million.

Yet the foundation's expansion has also been accompanied by financial problems. In 2007 and 2008, the foundation also found itself competing against Mrs. Clinton's presidential campaign for donors amid a recession. Millions of dollars in contributions intended to seed an endowment were diverted to other programs, creating tension between Mr. Magaziner and Mr. Band. The foundation piled up a $40 million deficit during those two years, according to tax returns. Last year, it ran more than $8 million in the red.

Amid those shortfalls, the foundation has sometimes catered to donors and celebrities who gave money in ways that raised eyebrows in the low-key nonprofit world. In 2009, during a Clinton Global Initiative gathering at the University of Texas at Austin, the foundation purchased a first-class ticket for the actress Natalie Portman, a special guest, who brought her beloved Yorkie, according to two former foundation employees.

In interviews, foundation officials partly blamed the 2008 recession and difficulties in getting donors to provide operating support rather than restricted grants for specific programs for the deficits.

But others criticized Mr. Magaziner, who is widely seen within the foundation as impulsive and lacking organizational skills. On one occasion, Mr. Magaziner dispatched a team of employees to fly around the world for months gathering ideas for a climate change proposal that never got off the ground. Another time, he ignored a report — which was commissioned at significant expense from the consulting firm McKinsey & Company — on how the foundation could get involved in forestry initiatives.

Mr. Magaziner's management style and difficulty keeping projects within budget were also raised in discussions that surrounded the 2011 Simpson Thacher review. One person who attended a meeting with Mr. Magaziner recalled his lying on a conference room table in the middle of the meeting because of terrible back spasms, snapping at a staff member.

Mr. Band repeatedly urged Mr. Clinton to fire Mr. Magaziner, according to people briefed on the matter. Mr. Clinton refused, confiding in aides that despite Mr. Magaziner's managerial weaknesses, he was a visionary with good intentions. The former president, according to one person who knows them both, "thinks Ira is brilliant — and brilliant people get away with a lot in Clinton world."

Indeed, by then, Mr. Magaziner had persuaded Mr. Clinton and the foundation to spin the health initiative off into a separate organization, with Mr. Magaziner as its chief executive and the Clinton Foundation appointing a majority of its board members. The financial problems continued. In 2010 and 2011, the first two years when the health initiative operated as a stand-alone organization, it ran annual shortfalls of more than $4 million. A new chief financial officer, hired in 2010, left eight months later.

A foundation official said the health initiative had only three chief financial officers in 10 years and that its financial problem was a common one in the nonprofit world: For all the grant money coming in — more than $160 million in 2011 — Mr. Magaziner had also had difficulty raising money for operating costs. But by the end of 2011, the health initiative had expanded its board, adding two seats.

Growing Ventures

As the foundation grew, so did the outside business ventures pursued by Mr. Clinton and several of his aides.None have drawn more scrutiny in Clinton circles than Teneo, a firm co-founded in 2009 by Mr. Band, described by some as a kind of surrogate son to Mr. Clinton. Aspiring to merge corporate consulting, public relations and merchant banking in a single business, Mr. Band poached executives from Wall Street, recruited other Clinton aides to join as employees or advisers and set up shop in a Midtown office formerly belonging to one of the country's top hedge funds.

By 2011, the firm had added a third partner, Declan Kelly, a former State Department envoy for Mrs. Clinton. And Mr. Clinton had signed up as a paid adviser to the firm.

Teneo worked on retainer, charging monthly fees as high as $250,000, according to current and former clients. The firm recruited clients who were also Clinton Foundation donors, while Mr. Band and Mr. Kelly encouraged others to become new foundation donors. Its marketing materials highlighted Mr. Band's relationship with Mr. Clinton and the Clinton Global Initiative, where Mr. Band sat on the board of directors through 2011 and remains an adviser. Some Clinton aides and foundation employees began to wonder where the foundation ended and Teneo began.

Those worries intensified after the collapse of MF Global, the international brokerage firm led by Jon S. Corzine, a former governor of New Jersey, in the fall of 2011. The firm had been among Teneo's earliest clients, and its collapse over bad European investments — while paying $125,000 a month for the firm's public relations and financial advice — drew Teneo and the Clintons unwanted publicity.

Mr. Clinton ended his advisory role with Teneo in March 2012, after an article appeared in The New York Post suggesting that Mrs. Clinton was angry over the MF Global controversy. A spokesman for Mr. Clinton denied the report. But in a statement released afterward, Mr. Clinton announced that he would no longer be paid by Teneo.

He also praised Mr. Band effusively, crediting him with keeping the foundation afloat and expressing hopes that Mr. Band would continue to advise the Global Initiative.

"I couldn't have accomplished half of what I have in my post-presidency without Doug Band," Mr. Clinton said in the statement.

Even that news release was a source of controversy within the foundation, according to two people with knowledge of the discussions. Mr. Band helped edit the statement, which other people around the Clintons felt gave him too much credit for the foundation's accomplishments.

Mr. Band left his paid position with the foundation in late 2010, but has remained involved with C.G.I., as have a number of Teneo clients, like Coca-Cola, Dow Chemical and UBS Americas. Standard Chartered, a British financial services company that paid a $340 million fine to New York regulators last year to settle charges that it had laundered money from Iran, is a Teneo client and a sponsor of the 2012 global initiative.

Last year, Coca-Cola's chief executive, Muhtar Kent, won a coveted spot on the dais with Mr. Clinton, discussing the company's partnership with another nonprofit to use its distributors to deliver medical goods to patients in Africa. A Coca-Cola spokesman said that the company's sponsorship of foundation initiatives long predated Teneo and that the firm plays no role in Coca-Cola's foundation work.

In March 2012, David Crane, the chief executive of NRG, an energy company, led a widely publicized trip with Mr. Clinton to Haiti, where they toured green energy and solar power projects that NRG finances through a $1 million commitment to the Clinton Global Initiative.

Officials said the Foundation has established clear guidelines for the Clinton Global Initiative to help prevent any favoritism or special treatment of particular donors or sponsors.

Teneo was not the only worry: other events thrust the foundation into internal turmoil. In 2011, a wave of midlevel program staff members departed, reflecting the frustration of much of the foundation's policy personnel with the old political hands running the organization. Around the time of the Simpson Thacher review, Mr. Lindsey suffered a stroke, underscoring concerns about the foundation's line of succession. John D. Podesta, a chief of staff in Mr. Clinton's White House, stepped in for several months as temporary chief executive.

Chelsea

While much attention has focused on Ms. Clinton's emerging role within the foundation, advisers to the family say her daughter's growing involvement could prove more critical in the years ahead. After years of pursuing other career paths, including working at McKinsey & Company and a hedge fund, Ms. Clinton, 33, has begun to assert herself as a force within the foundation. Her perspective is shaped far more than her parents' by her time in the world of business, and she is poised to play a significant role in shaping the foundation's future, particularly if Mrs. Clinton chooses to run for president.

She formally joined the foundation's board in 2011, marking her growing role there — and the start of intensifying tensions between her and Mr. Band. Several people close to the Clintons said that she became increasingly concerned with the negative impact Mr. Band's outside business might have on her father's work and that she cited concerns raised during the internal review about potential conflicts of interest involving Teneo.

It was Ms. Clinton who suggested that the newly installed chief executive, Eric Braverman, be considered for the job during a nearly two-year search. A friend and a former colleague from McKinsey, Mr. Braverman, 38, had helped the Clintons with philanthropic projects in Haiti after the earthquake there. And his hiring coincided with Ms. Clinton's appointment as the vice chairwoman of the foundation board, where she will bear significant responsibility for steering her family's philanthropy, both in the causes it tackles and in the potential political and financial conflicts it must avoid.

Ms. Clinton has also grown worried that the foundation she stood to inherit would collapse without her father, who turns 67 next week. Mr. Clinton, who had quadruple-bypass surgery in 2004 and no longer eats meat or dairy products, talks frequently about his own mortality.

Mr. Catsimatidis said Ms. Clinton "has to learn how to deal with the whole world because she wants to follow in the footsteps of her father and her mother."

"Corporate" Hillary

Assuming Hillary Clinton runs for president in 2016, much of her popular support will be based on her image as an advocate of women's rights. During her 2008 candidacy, the National Organization of Women (NOW) endorsed Clinton based on her "long history of support for women's empowerment." A group of 250 academics and activists calling themselves "Feminists for Clinton" praised her "powerful, inspiring advocacy of the human rights of women" and her "enormous contributions" as a policymaker.

Since then, NOW and other mainstream women's organizations have been eagerly anticipating her 2016 candidacy. Clinton and supporters have recently stepped up efforts to portray her as a champion of both women's and LGBT rights.

Such depictions have little basis in Clinton's past performance. While she has indeed spoken about gender and sexual rights with considerable frequency, and while she may not share the overtly misogynistic and anti-LGBT views of most Republican politicians, as a policymaker she has consistently favored policies devastating to women and LGBT persons.

Why, then, does she continue to enjoy such support from self-identified feminists? Part of the answer surely lies in the barrage of sexist attacks that have targeted her and the understandable desire of many feminists to see a woman president. But that's not the whole story. We suggest that feminist enthusiasm for Hillary Clinton is reflective of a profound crisis of U.S. liberal feminism, which has long embraced or accepted corporate capitalism, racism, empire, and even heterosexism and transphobia.

Making Profit and War

All issues of wealth, power, and violence are also women's and LGBT rights issues. For instance, neoliberal economic policies of austerity and privatization disproportionately hurt women and LGBT individuals, who are often the lowest paid and the first workers to be fired, the most likely to bear the burdens of family maintenance, and the most affected by the involuntary migration, domestic violence, homelessness, and mental illness that are intensified by poverty.

Hillary Clinton's record on such issues is hardly encouraging. Her decades of service on corporate boards and in major policy roles as First Lady, U.S. Senator and Secretary of State give a clear indication of where she stands. One of Clinton's first high-profile public positions was at Walmart, where she served on the board from 1986 to 1992. She "remained silent" in board meetings as her company "waged a major campaign against labor unions seeking to represent store workers," as an ABC review of video recordings later noted.

Clinton recounted in her 2003 book that Walmart CEO Sam Walton "taught me a great deal about corporate integrity and success." Though she later began trying to shed her public identification with the company in order to attract labor support for her Senate and presidential candidacies, Walmart executives have continued to look favorably on her, with Alice Walton donating the maximum amount to the "Ready for Hillary" Super PAC in 2013. Walton's $25,000 donation was considerably higher than the average annual salary for Walmart's hourly employees, two-thirds of whom are women.

After leaving Walmart, Clinton became perhaps the most active First Lady in history. While it would be unfair to hold her responsible for all her husband's policies, she did play a significant role in shaping and justifying many of them.

In her 2003 memoir she boasted of gutting welfare: "By the time Bill and I left the White House, welfare rolls had dropped 60 percent" — and not because poverty had dropped. Women and children, the main recipients of welfare, have been the primary victims. Jeffrey St. Clair at Counterpunch notes that prior to the welfare reform, "more than 70 percent of poor families with children received some kind of cash assistance. By 2010, less than 30 percent got any kind of cash aid and the amount of the benefit had declined by more than 50 percent from pre-reform levels."

Clinton also lobbied Congress to pass her husband's deeply racist crime bill, which, observes Michelle Alexander in The New Jim Crow, "escalated the drug war beyond what conservatives had imagined possible," expanding mass incarceration and the death penalty.

Arguably the two most defining features of Clinton's tenures as Senator (2001-2009) and Secretary of State (2009-2013) were her promotion of U.S. corporate profit-making and her aggressive assertion of the U.S. government's right to intervene in foreign countries. Reflecting on this performance as Clinton left her Secretary post in January 2013, Bloomberg Businessweek commented that "Clinton turned the State Department into a machine for promoting U.S. business." She sought "to install herself as the government's highest-ranking business lobbyist," directly negotiating lucrative overseas contracts for U.S. corporations like Boeing, Lockheed, and General Electric. Not surprisingly, "Clinton's corporate cheerleading has won praise from business groups."

Clinton herself has been very honest about this aim, albeit not when speaking in front of progressives. Her 2011 Foreign Policy essay on "America's Pacific Century" spoke at length about the objective of "opening new markets for American businesses," containing no fewer than ten uses of the phrases "open markets," "open trade," and permutations thereof.

A major focus of this effort is the Trans-Pacific Partnership involving twelve Pacific countries that is now being negotiated secretively by the Obama administration with the assistance of over 600 corporate "advisors." Like Bill Clinton's NAFTA, the deal is intended to further empower multinational corporations at the expense of workers, consumers, and the environment in all countries involved. Lower wages and increased rates of displacement, detention, and physical violence for female and LGBT populations are among the likely consequences, given the results of existing "free-trade" agreements.

Clinton's article also elaborated on the role of U.S. military power in advancing these economic goals. The past "growth" of eastern Asia has depended on "the security and stability that has long been guaranteed by the U.S. military," and "a more broadly distributed military presence across the region will provide vital advantages" in the future.

Clinton thus reaffirmed the bipartisan consensus on the U.S. right to use military force abroad in pursuit of economic interest — echoing, for instance, her husband's Secretary of Defense William Cohen, who in 1999 reserved the right to "the unilateral use of military power" in the name of "ensuring uninhibited access to key markets, energy supplies, and strategic resources."

In the Middle East and Central Asia, Clinton has likewise defended the U.S. right to violate international law and human rights. As Senator she not only voted in favor of the illegal 2003 U.S. invasion of Iraq — a monstrous crime that has killed hundreds of thousands of people while sowing terror and sectarianism across the region — she was an outspoken advocate of the invasion and a fierce critic of resistance within the United Nations.

Since then she has only partially disavowed that position (out of political expediency) while speaking in paternalistic and racist terms about Iraqis. Senator Clinton was an especially staunch supporter — even by the standards of the U.S. Congress — of Israel's illegal military actions and settlement activity in the Occupied Palestinian Territories.

As Barack Obama's Secretary of State, she presided over the expansion of illegal drone attacks that by conservative estimates have killed many hundreds of civilians, while reaffirming U.S. alliances with vicious dictatorships. As she recounts in her 2014 memoir Hard Choices, "In addition to our work with the Israelis, the Obama Administration also increased America's own sea and air presence in the Persian Gulf and deepened our ties to the Gulf monarchies."

Clinton herself is widely recognized to have been one of the administration's most forceful advocates of attacking or expanding military operations in Afghanistan, Libya and Syria and of strengthening U.S. ties to dictatorships in Tunisia, Egypt, Yemen, Bahrain, Morocco and elsewhere. Maybe the women and girls of these countries, including those whose lives have been destroyed by U.S. bombs, can take comfort in knowing that a "feminist" helped craft U.S. policy.

Secretary Clinton and her team worked to ensure that any challenges to U.S.-Israeli domination of the Middle East were met with brute force and/or various forms of collective punishment. On Iran, she often echoes the bipartisan line that "all options must remain on the table" — a flagrant violation of the UN Charter's prohibition of "the threat or use of force" in international relations — and brags in Hard Choices that her team "successfully campaigned around the world to impose crippling sanctions" on the country.

She ensured that Palestine's UN statehood bid "went nowhere in the Security Council." Though out of office by the time of Israel's savage 2014 assault on Gaza, she ardently defended it in interviews. This context helps explain her recent praise for Henry Kissinger, renowned for bombing civilians and supporting regimes that killed and tortured hundreds of thousands of suspected dissidents. She writes in the Washington Post that she "relied on his counsel when I served as secretary of state."

Militarization and Its Benefits

In another domain of traditional U.S. ownership, Latin America, Clinton also seems to have followed Kissinger's example. As confirmed in her 2014 book, she effectively supported the 2009 military overthrow of left-of-center Honduran President Manuel Zelaya — a "caricature of a Central American strongman" — by pushing for a "compromise" solution that endorsed his illegal ouster.

She has advocated the application of the Colombia model — highly militarized "anti-drug" initiatives coupled with neoliberal economic policies — to other countries in the region, and is full of praise for the devastating militarization of Mexico over the past decade. In Mexico that model has resulted in 80,000 or more deaths since 2006, including the 43 Mexican student activists disappeared (and presumably massacred) in September 2014.

In the Caribbean, the U.S. model of choice is Haiti, where Clinton and her husband have relentlessly promoted the sweatshop model of production since the 1990s. WikiLeaks documents show that in 2009 her State Department collaborated with subcontractors for Hanes, Levi's, and Fruit of the Loom to oppose a minimum wage increase for Haitian workers. After the January 2010 earthquake she helped spearhead the highly militarized U.S. response.

Militarization has plentiful benefits, as Clinton understands. It can facilitate corporate investment, such as the "gold rush" that the U.S. ambassador described following the Haiti earthquake. It can keep in check nonviolent dissidents, such as hungry Haitian workers or leftist students in Mexico. And it can help combat the influence of countries like Venezuela which have challenged neoliberalism and U.S. geopolitical control.

These goals have long motivated U.S. hostility toward Cuba, and thus Clinton's recent call for ending the U.S. embargo against Cuba was pragmatic, not principled: "It wasn't achieving its goals" of overthrowing the government, as she says in her recent book. The goal there, as in Venezuela, is to compel the country to "restore private property and return to a free market economy," as she demanded of Venezuela in 2010.

A reasonable synopsis of Clinton's record around the world comes from neoconservative policy advisor Robert Kagan, who, like Clinton, played an important role in advocating the 2003 Iraq invasion. "I feel comfortable with her on foreign policy," Kagan told the New York Times last June.

Asked what to expect from a Hillary Clinton presidency, Kagan predicted that "[i]f she pursues a policy which we think she will pursue, it's something that might have been called neocon." But — he added — "clearly her supporters are not going to call it that; they are going to call it something else."

Wall Street

Down on Wall Street they don't believe (Clinton's populist rhetoric) for a minute. While the finance industry does genuinely hate Warren, the big bankers love Clinton, and by and large they badly want her to be president. Many of the rich and powerful in the financial industry—among them, Goldman Sachs CEO Lloyd Blankfein, Morgan Stanley CEO James Gorman, Tom Nides, a powerful vice chairman at Morgan Stanley, and the heads of JP MorganChase and Bank of America—consider Clinton a pragmatic problem-solver not prone to populist rhetoric. To them, she's someone who gets the idea that we all benefit if Wall Street and American business thrive. They dismiss it quickly as political maneuvers. None of them think she really means her populism.

The consensus on Wall Street is that she is running—and running hard—and that her national organization is quickly falling into place behind the scenes. That all makes her attractive. Wall Street, above all, loves a winner, especially one who is not likely to tamper too radically with its vast money pot.

Clinton's rock-solid support on Wall Street is not anything that can be dislodged based on a few seemingly off-the-cuff comments in Boston calculated to protect her left flank. Most people in New York on the finance side view her as being very pragmatic.

Women's & LGBT Rights

What about Clinton's record on that narrower set of issues more commonly associated with women's and LGBT rights — control over one's reproductive system and freedom from discrimination and sexual violence?

Perhaps the best that can be said is that Clinton does not espouse the medieval view of female bodily autonomy shared by most Republicans, and does not actively encourage homophobia and transphobia. She has consistently said that abortion should remain legal (but "rare") and that birth control should be widely available, and when in office generally acted in accord with those statements. She has recently voiced support for gay marriage rights. These positions are worth something, even if they are mainly a reflection of pressure from below.

But nor does her record on these rights merit glowing praise. In addition to partly capitulating to the far-right anti-choice agenda in Congress, with disproportionate harm to low-income parents, Clinton and other Democrats have also actively undermined these rights. Some observers have argued that Clinton's repetition of the Democratic slogan that abortion should be "safe, legal, and rare" reinforces the stigmatization of those who choose that option.

Her narrow definition of reproductive rights — as abortion and contraception only — does not allow much in the way of material support for parents or young children. She insists that abortion must remain "rare," but has also helped deprive poor expecting parents of the financial support they would need to raise a child (for instance, through the 1996 welfare reform and the fiscal austerity regarding social programs that has become the bipartisan consensus in Washington). She has supported the further militarization of the Mexico border and the arrest of undocumented immigrants, undermining the reproductive rights of women who give birth in chains in detention centers before being deported back to lives of poverty and violence.

Regarding non-discrimination, Clinton's record is also worse than her reputation suggests. Her old company Walmart, widely accused of discriminating against women employees, was recently praised by the Clinton Foundation for its "efforts to empower girls and women."

Clinton has given little serious indication that she opposes discrimination against LGBT individuals in the workplace (which is still legal in the majority of U.S. states). Her very recent reversal of her opposition to gay marriage came only after support for the idea has become politically beneficial and perhaps necessary for Democrats. At best, Clinton in these respects has been a cautious responder to progressive political winds rather than a trailblazing leader.

Clinton's foreign policy record is even more at odds with her reputation as a champion of women's and LGBT rights. Her policy of support for the 2009 coup in Honduras has been disastrous for both groups.

Violent hate crimes against LGBT Hondurans have skyrocketed. In mid-2014, leading LGBT activist Nelson Arambú reported 176 murders against LGBT individuals since 2009, an average of about 35 per year, compared to just over one per year in the period 1994-2009.

Arambú located this violence within the broader human rights nightmare of post-coup Honduras, noting the contributions of U.S.-funded militarization and the post-coup regimes' pattern of "shutting down government institutions charged with promoting and protecting the human rights of vulnerable sectors of the population — such as women, children, indigenous communities, and Afro-Hondurans." Clinton has been worse than silent on the situation, actively supporting and praising the post-coup governments.

In a review of her work as Secretary of State, Middle East scholar Stephen Zunes concludes that while "Hillary Clinton has been more outspoken than any previous Secretary of State regarding the rights of women and sexual minorities," this position is "more rhetoric than reality."

As one example he points to the U.S.-backed monarchy in Morocco, which has long occupied Western Sahara with U.S. support. Two weeks after Secretary Clinton publicly praised the dictatorship for having "protected and expanded" women's rights, a teenage girl named Amina Filali committed suicide by taking rat poison. Filali had been raped at age 15 and then "forced to marry her rapist, who subsequently battered and abused her."

Although Clinton's liberal supporters are likely to lament such details as exceptions within an impressive overall record ("She's still much better than a Republican!"), it is quite possible that her actions have harmed feminist movements worldwide. As Zunes argues:

"Given Clinton's backing of neo-liberal economic policies and war-making by the United States and its allies, her advocacy of women's rights overseas...may have actually set back indigenous feminist movements in the same way that the Bush administration's 'democracy-promotion' agenda was a serious setback to popular struggles for freedom and democracy....Hillary Clinton's call for greater respect for women's rights in Muslim countries never had much credibility while US-manufactured ordinance is blowing up women in Lebanon, Gaza, Iraq, Afghanistan and Pakistan."

Threading Needles

This summary of Clinton's "enormous contributions" (Feminists for Clinton) is just a partial sampling. On almost all other major issues, from climate change to immigration to education to financial regulation, President Hillary Clinton would likely be no better than President Obama, if not worse.

As with Obama, it is of course necessary for Clinton to "call it something else," in Robert Kagan's words. The stark disjunction between rhetoric and policies reflects a well understood logic. Mainstream U.S. political candidates, particularly Democrats, must find ways to attract popular support while simultaneously reassuring corporate and financial elites.

The latter, for their part, usually understand the need for a good dose of "populism" during a campaign, and accept it as long as it stays within certain bounds and is not reflected in policy itself. One former aide to Bill Clinton, speaking to The Hill last July, compared this rhetorical strategy to threading a needle, saying that "good politicians — and I think Hillary is a good politician — are good at threading needles, and I think there's probably a way to do it."

Hillary Clinton faces the challenge of convincing voters that she is a champion of "people historically excluded," as she claims in her 2014 memoir. The Hill reported that "Clinton is now test-driving various campaign themes," including the familiar progressive promises to "increase upward mobility" and "decrease inequality."

Her memoirs, for those who dare to suffer through them, include invocations of dead leftists like Frederick Douglass, Harriet Tubman, and Martin Luther King, Jr.

This public relations work requires that her past record be hidden from view, lest it create a credibility problem. Here Clinton has enjoyed the assistance of many liberal feminists. One former Obama staffer, speaking to The Hill, notes Clinton's successful efforts "to co-opt the base groups in the past eight years."

Rhetoric is not totally meaningless. The extent to which politicians like Clinton have been compelled to portray themselves — however cynically — as champions of the rights of workers, women, LGBT people, and other "historically excluded" groups is an indication that popular pressures for those rights have achieved substantial force. In the case of LGBT rights this rhetorical shift is very recent, and reflects a growth in the movement's power that is to be celebrated.

But taking politicians' rhetoric at face value is one of the gravest errors that a progressive can make.

The Feminists Not Invited

Liberal feminists' support of Hillary Clinton is not just due to credulousness, though. It also reflects a narrowness of analysis, vision, and values. In this country feminism is often understood as the right of women — wealthy white women most of all — to share in the spoils of corporate capitalism and U.S. imperial power. By not confronting the exclusion of non-whites, foreigners, working-class people, and other groups from this vision, liberal feminists miss a crucial opportunity to create a more inclusive, more powerful movement.

Alternative currents within the feminist movement, both here and globally, have long rejected this impoverished understanding of feminism. For them, feminism means confronting patriarchy but also capitalism, imperialism, white supremacy and other forms of oppression that interlock with and reinforce patriarchy. It means fighting to replace a system in which the rights of people and other living things are systematically subordinated to the quest for profits. It means fighting so that all people — everywhere on the gender, sexual and body spectrum — can enjoy basic rights like food, health care, housing, a safe and clean environment, and control over their bodies, labor and identities.

This more holistic feminist vision is apparent all around the world, including among the women of places like Pakistan, Afghanistan, and Iran, whose oppression is constantly evoked by Western leaders to justify war and occupation. The courageous Pakistani teenager Malala Yousafzai, awarded the Nobel Peace Prize for her feminist advocacy, has also criticized illegal U.S. drone attacks for killing civilians and aiding terrorist recruitment.

Yousafzai's opposition to the Taliban won her adoring Western media coverage and an invitation to the Obama White House, but her criticism of drones has gone virtually unmentioned. Also unmentioned are her comments about socialism, which she says "is the only answer" to "free us from the chains of bigotry and exploitation."

The Revolutionary Association of the Women of Afghanistan (RAWA) has equally opposed the Taliban, U.S.-backed fundamentalist forces, and the U.S. occupation. While liberal groups like Feminist Majority have depicted the U.S. war as a noble crusade to protect Afghan women, RAWA says that the United States "has empowered and equipped the most traitorous, anti-democratic, misogynist and corrupt fundamentalist gangs in Afghanistan," merely "replacing one fundamentalist regime with another."

The logic is simple: U.S. elites prefer the "bloody and suffocating rule of Afghanistan" by fundamentalist warlords "to an independent, pro-democracy and pro-women's rights government" that might jeopardize "its interests in the region." Women's liberation, RAWA emphasizes, "can be achieved only by the people of Afghanistan and by democracy-loving forces through a hard, decisive and long struggle". Needless to say, Clinton and Obama have not invited the RAWA women to Washington.

A group of Iranian and Iranian-American feminists, the Raha Iranian Feminist Collective, takes a similar position in relation to their own country. In 2011 it bitterly condemned the Ahmadinejad regime's systematic violations ofwomen's rights (and those of other groups), but just as forcefully condemned "all forms of US intervention," including the "crippling sanctions" that Hillary Clinton is so proud of her role in implementing. The group said that sanctions "further immiserate the very people they claim to be helping," and noted that few if any genuine grassroots voices in Iran had "called for or supported the US/UN/EU sanctions."

In Latin America, too, many working-class feminists argue that the fight for gender and sexual liberation is inseparable from the struggles for self-determination and a just economic system. Speaking to NACLA Report on the Americas, Venezuelan organizer Yanahir Reyes recently lauded "all of the social policy" that has "focused on liberating women" under Hugo Chávez and NicolásMaduro, those evil autocrats so despised by Hillary Clinton.

Reyes emphasized the importance of independent feminist organizing: "Women from the feminist struggle have effectively brought to light the importance of dismantling a patriarchal system," thus pushing Chavismo in a more feminist direction. "It is a very hard internal fight," says Reyes, but "this is the space where we can achieve it" — under a government sympathetic to socialism, "not in a different form of government."

This tradition of more holistic feminisms is not absent from the United States. In the 19th century, Black women like Ida B. Wells and Sojourner Truth linked the struggles for abolition and suffrage and denounced the lynching campaigns that murdered Black men and women in the name of "saving" white women. In contrast, leaders of the white suffrage movement like Elizabeth Cady Stanton and Susan B. Anthony refused to include people of color in the struggle for citizenship rights.

Unfortunately this history continues to be distorted. In 2008 Gloria Steinem, the standard bearer of liberal feminism, said that she supported Clinton's campaign over Obama's in part because "Black men were given the vote a half-century before women of any race were allowed to mark a ballot."

The assumption that all women are equally oppressed by patriarchy (and that all men are equal oppressors) was fiercely challenged by U.S. women of color, working-class women, and lesbians in the 1970s and 1980s. Feminists of color analyzed their gender and sexual oppression within the larger history of U.S. slavery, capitalism, and empire.

In New York the women of the Young Lords Party pushed their organization to denounce forced sterilizations of women of color, to demand safe and accessible abortion and contraception, and to call for community-controlled clinics. They redefined reproductive rights as the right to abortion and contraception and the right to have children without living in poverty.

In recent years, a radical LGBT movement has fought for reforms like marriage equality while also moving beyond marriage and condemning how the state, from prisons to the military, is the biggest perpetrator of violence against gender and sexual non-conforming peoples, particularly trans women of color and undocumented queers.

These queer radicals reject the logic that casts the United States and Israel as tolerant while characterizing occupied territories, from U.S. to Palestinian ghettoes, as inherently homophobic and in need of military and other outside intervention. They condemn U.S. wars and the Obama administration's persecution of whistleblowers like Manning (who helped expose, among other U.S. crimes, military orders to ignore the sexual abuse of Iraqi detainees and the trafficking of Afghan children).

A more robust vision of feminism doesn't mean that we shouldn't defend women like Hillary Clinton against sexist attacks — we should, just as we defend Barack Obama against racist ones. But it does mean that we must listen to the voices of the most marginalized women and gender and sexual minorities — many of whom are extremely critical of Clintonite feminism — and act in solidarity with movements that seek equity in all realms of life and for all people. These are the feminists not invited to the Hillary Clinton party, except perhaps to serve and clean up

State Departement

In her book, "Hard Choices," Mrs. Clinton said one of her goals at the State Department was "placing economics at the heart of our foreign policy." She wrote: "It was clearer than ever that America's economic strength and our global leadership were a package deal."

Matthew Goodman, a former Clinton State Department official who is now at the Center for Strategic and International Studies, a Washington think tank, says Mrs. Clinton is the first secretary of state to make economics such a focus since George C. Marshall, who helped rebuild postwar Europe.

That approach, which Mrs. Clinton called "economic statecraft," emerged in discussions with Robert Hormats, a former Goldman Sachs Group. The focus positioned Mrs. Clinton to pursue not just foreign-policy results, but domestic economic ones.

Early in Mrs. Clinton's tenure, according to Mr. Hormats, Microsoft's then Chief Research Officer Craig Mundie asked the State Department to send a ranking official to a fourth annual meeting of U.S. software executives and Chinese government officials about piracy and Internet freedom. Mr. Hormats joined the December 2009 meeting in Beijing.

Since 2005, Microsoft has given the Clinton Global Initiative $1.3 million, in addition to free software, according to the foundation.

In 2011, Microsoft launched a three-year initiative coordinated by the Clinton Global Initiative to provide free or discounted software and other resources to students and teachers—a commitment Microsoft estimated to be worth $130 million.

Mr. Hormats says there was no relation between Microsoft's donations and the State Department's participation in the China conference.

In 2012, the Clinton Foundation approached GE about working together to expand a health-access initiative the company had launched four years earlier, says a GE spokeswoman.

That same year, Mrs. Clinton lobbied for GE to be selected by the Algerian government to build power plants in that country. She went to Algiers that October and met with President AbdelazizBouteflika. "I saw an opportunity for advancing prosperity in Algeria and seizing an opportunity for American business," she explained in her book.

A month after Mrs. Clinton's trip, the Clinton Foundation announced the health-initiative partnership with GE, the company's first involvement with the foundation. GE eventually contributed between $500,000 and $1 million to the partnership.

The following September, GE won the contracts with the Algerian government, saying they marked "some of its largest power agreements in company history."

Mrs. Clinton championed U.S. energy companies and launched an office to promote overseas projects. Many of those efforts were focused in Eastern and Central Europe, where she saw energy development as a hedge against Russia's dominance in oil and gas. Companies that had interests in those areas included Exxon Mobil and Chevron Corp.

One effort, the Global Shale Gas Initiative, promoted hydraulic fracturing, or fracking, a technique perfected by U.S. companies. In 2010, Mrs. Clinton flew to Krakow to announce a Polish-American cooperation on a global shale-gas initiative, according to her book. At the time, the U.S. Energy Information Administration predicted abundant deposits of shale gas in Poland.

After pursuing shale-gas projects in Poland, Exxon Mobil gave up a few years later, and Chevron said late last month it would abandon its Poland project.

In 2012, Mrs. Clinton flew to Sofia, Bulgaria, and urged the Bulgarian Parliament to reconsider its moratorium on fracking and its withdrawal of Chevron's five-year exploration license. A few months later, the government allowed conventional gas exploration, but not fracking. Chevron left Bulgaria in 2012.

Ben Schreiber of the environmental group Friends of the Earth says: "We've long been concerned about the ties that Hillary Clinton has to the oil-and-gas industry."

Both Exxon and Chevron are supporters of the Clinton Foundation. Chevron donated $250,000 in 2013. A Chevron spokesman said the Clinton charity "is one of many programs and partnerships that the company has had or maintains across a number of issue areas and topics pertinent to our business."

Exxon Mobil has given about $2 million to the Clinton Global Initiative, starting in 2009. Since 2007, Exxon Mobil also has given $16.8 million to Vital Voices, the nonprofit women's group co-founded by Mrs. Clinton, according to the group's spokeswoman.

An Exxon Mobil spokesman said the donations were made to support work on issues Exxon Mobil has long championed, such as programs to fight malaria and empower women. "That is the sole motivation for our support of charitable programs associated with the Clintons," he said. "We did not seek or receive any special consideration on the Shale Gas Initiative."

In October 2009, Mrs. Clinton went to bat for aerospace giant Boeing, which was seeking to sell jets to Russia, by flying to Moscow to visit the Boeing Design Center. "I made the case that Boeing's jets set the global gold standard, and, after I left, our embassy kept at it," she wrote in her book.

About seven months later, in June 2010, Russia agreed to purchase 50 Boeing 737s for $3.7 billion, choosing Boeing over Europe's Airbus Group.

Two months later, Boeing made its first donation to the Clinton Foundation—$900,000 to help rebuild Haiti's public-education system. Overall, Boeing has contributed around $1.1 million to the Clinton Foundation since 2010.

A Boeing spokeswoman said it is routine for U.S. officials to advocate on behalf of businesses such as Boeing. "U.S. businesses face fierce global competition, and oftentimes an unlevel playing field in the global marketplace," she said in a written statement. "Secretary Clinton did nothing for Boeing that former U.S. presidents and cabinet secretaries haven't done for decades, or that their foreign counterparts haven't done on behalf of companies like Airbus."

Before every overseas trip, says Mr. Hormats, the former undersecretary of state, he helped prepare a list of U.S. corporate interests for Mrs. Clinton to advocate while abroad.

During Mrs. Clinton's three trips to India, she urged the government to kill a ban on stores that sell multiple brands, a law aimed at department stores or big-box retailers such as Wal-Mart Stores Inc.

"It wasn't just Wal-Mart," Mr. Hormats says. "It was the whole point of multibrand retail. Wal-Mart was, of course, the biggest."

Mrs. Clinton served on the board of the Bentonville, Ark.-based retailer between 1986 and 1992, when her husband was governor of that state, and the law firm she worked for at the time represented the company. Wal-Mart has donated nearly $1.2 million to the Clinton Foundation for a program that issues grants to student-run charitable projects. The company also has paid more than $370,000 in membership fees to the foundation since 2008, according to a Wal-Mart spokesman.

Trip to India

Before Mrs. Clinton's official trip to India in 2012, Wal-Mart Chief Executive Mike Duke joined her at the Summit of the Americas in Cartagena, Colombia, to pledge $12 million to help women in Latin America. The donation included $1.5 million in grants to 55,000 women entrepreneurs through the International Fund for Women and Girls, one of the 15 public-private partnerships Mrs. Clinton created at the State Department, and $500,000 for Vital Voices, the charity she co-founded.

"We committed to helping women around the world live better," Mr. Duke said at the time. "By working with leaders like Secretary Clinton, we're bringing that mission to life."

One month later, Mrs. Clinton traveled to India to make the case against the ban on retail stores such as Wal-Mart. Then-Prime Minister Manmohan Singh had proposed allowing companies such as Wal-Mart to invest up to 51% directly in local multibrand retailers, but one of his allies, Mamata Banerjee, a regional governor, opposed the idea. Ms. Banerjee's support was key to Mr. Singh's majority in Parliament.

Mrs. Clinton met with Ms. Banerjee to press the matter. She also said in a speech in West Bengal that U.S. retailers could bring an "enormous amount of expertise" to India in areas ranging from supply-chain management to working with small producers and farmers. Her lobbying was unsuccessful.

A Wal-Mart spokesman said the retailer had lobbied the State Department on the issue, which he said was one of dozens of topics important to the business.

After Mrs. Clinton's India trip, her husband asked Mr. Duke, Walmart's CEO, to change his schedule to appear at the opening panel of the Clinton Global Initiative. Mr. Duke agreed.

Hillary served as US senator from New York from 2001 to 2009, but her accomplishments are thin. No piece of legislation bears her name. Her tenure came to be defined in the 2008 presidential primaries by her vote for the war in Iraq — which Barack Obama, who had opposed the war, used to chip away at her foreign policy bona fides.

Her accomplishments as secretary of state are as unclear. She traveled to 112 countries, but again, she has nothing of consequence to her name: no peace treaty, no accord, no summit of consequence. Her defenders say she helped restore America's reputation in the wake of the wars in Iraq and Afghanistan; critics say she was too afraid to make a mistake that would affect her presidential run in 2016.

When asked in 2014 by Diane Sawyer to name her greatest achievement or "signature doctrine," Hillary could not. "We haven't had a doctrine since containment worked with the Soviet Union," she said. "But we've had presidents who've made some tough calls and some hard choices, some of which have worked, and some of which have not."

That approach, which Mrs. Clinton called "economic statecraft," emerged in discussions with Robert Hormats, a former Goldman Sachs Group Inc. investment banker who has worked in Democratic and Republican administrations and became an undersecretary of state. "One of the very first items was, how do we strengthen the role of the State Department in economic policy?" he says.

Early in Mrs. Clinton's tenure, according to Mr. Hormats, Microsoft's then Chief Research Officer Craig Mundie asked the State Department to send a ranking official to a fourth annual meeting of U.S. software executives and Chinese government officials about piracy and Internet freedom. Mr. Hormats joined the December 2009 meeting in Beijing.

Mr. Hormats says there was no relation between Microsoft's donations and the State Department's participation in the China conference.

Before every overseas trip, says Mr. Hormats, the former undersecretary of state, he helped prepare a list of U.S. corporate interests for Mrs. Clinton to advocate while abroad.

Benghazi

A trail of emails appears to shed yet more light on the Benghazi cover-up story that continues to nag President Obama and then Secretary of State and current Democratic presidential hopeful Hillary Clinton. The latest exposure indicates that both Obama and Clinton knew that UN Secretary Susan Rice's claim to the press that the attack on the Benghazi compound killing Libyan Ambassador Christopher Stevens and three other Americans was due to an anti-Muslim youtube video was a complete lie.

This latest piece of incriminating evidence is what Republicans are now calling their "smoking gun" despite months that have stretched into years of the Congressional investigation led by Representative Darrel Issa (R-CA). His so called investigation that was supposed to uncover the truth behind that fateful day of September 11th, 2012 has often been labeled "a witch hunt" by Democrats and supporters of Obama and Hillary Clinton.

This week's news may be the needed breakthrough that will ultimately lead to the unveiling of what many critics of the Obama administration have been claiming all along. And that is Obama and Hillary purposely withheld the truth from the American public for fear that it would derail Obama's reelection less than two months after the death of the four Americans in Benghazi. In retrospect now Obama's rush to war in Syria last September is far better understood when taking a hard look at the 2012 Benghazi embassy attack.

The so called Arab spring uprising revolts in Middle Eastern and North African nations in fact have been the result of covert manipulation by the CIA. After getting rid of our one time allies in Iraq's Saddam Hussein and Egypt's Hosni Mubarak, next on the US regime-change hit list came Libya's Muammar Gaddafi. In 2007 retired General Wesley Clark revealed a neocon plan he became privy to a couple weeks after 9/11 of the ambitious Bush administration agenda to take down seven sovereign governments in the next five years that included Afghanistan, Iraq, Sudan, Somalia, Libya, Syria and Iran.

With gusto President Obama inherited this same agenda and proceeded to finish the job in removing Libya's longtime dictator Gaddafi. And so began the NATO air bombardment of Libya killing many innocent victims that softened the resistance to an all out assault on Gaddafi's military forces largely spearheaded by al Qaeda mercenaries from all over the Middle East as well as native Libyan al Qaeda affiliated militia groups, some from Benghazi.

In the spring of 2011 even prior to Gaddafi's capture and killing, as an envoy to the rebel coalition the future Libyan Ambassador Christopher Stevens was sent to Benghazi, a city in eastern Libya that has long been a hotbed of Islamic extremism that includes various Al Qaeda affiliated groups and militias. Stevens spoke Arabic and had twenty years of foreign diplomatic service experience when he was selected to become the Ambassador after the fall of the Gaddafi government. The State Department resent him to work back in Benghazi rather than the Libyan capitol Tripoli to assist the area's transition to the new puppet government the US had installed.

But because Benghazi and eastern Libya had a history of resisting national governance, Stevens faced an uphill struggle and near impossible task. Beginning in June of 2012, a full three months prior to the Benghazi embassy compound attack that killed the Ambassador and three other Americans, Stevens' requests for increased security began falling on deaf ears in Washington. Stevens' boss, Secretary of State Hillary Clinton, failed to heed any of his increasingly urgent calls. Just days prior to the embassy onslaught, the British consulate had been attacked and all its diplomatic staff were safely evacuated away.

Last year efforts to blame Stevens for irresponsibly turning down security offered in Benghazi were anonymously leaked, insisting that the ambassador twice had turned down offers of increased military security from AFRICOM commander General Ham.

For obvious reasons the now retired general refuses to discuss what he knew or did not know of the events leading up to the Benghazi attack. However, throughout the aftermath of the Americans' deaths, Stevens' own deputy ambassador Gregory Hicks in Tripoli has maintained that he never knew of any such alleged offers made to Stevens for more security.

Since the strategy targeting Ambassador Stevens as the sole reason for the lack of security at his embassy compound clearly backfired, a whitewashed report was released last year by the Accountability Review Board. The two men behind this report are Hillary's buddies Ambassador Pickering and former Joint Chiefs of Staff Admiral Mullens. Thus no surprise that they decided from the outset that it would not be necessary to even bother to interview Hillary, satisfied to blame it on lower level State Department bureaucrats' error in judgment not to supply adequate security. The alleged failure to authorize proper military security was because the Benghazi compound was relegated to being a temporary outpost. Of course this is just another feeble attempt to shield Queen Hillary who sent Stevens herself to Benghazi fully aware of it being an al Qaeda trouble spot.

But Benghazi under the cover of the State Department was ideal for the covert CIA and Joint Special Operations Command (JSOC) needed to coordinate arms smuggling that Obama, Hillary and then CIA Director Petraeus were knee deep in. Stevens ultimately may have felt he was being used as the convenient decoy for the clandestine activity he wanted no part of.

Years earlier as a former Peace Corps volunteer and a seasoned career diplomat, becoming a lookout for an immoral criminal gun running operation may not have been what he had signed on for as the Libyan Ambassador. Thus, he very likely voiced his objection to what his bosses in Washington were misusing him for, and as vindictive and petty as Obama and Hillary are, Stevens was likely punished for not going along with their program.

Hence, all his urgent pleas that began as early as June 2012, a full three months prior to the September attack, requesting increased security were ignored, including his desperate cry for help moments before his murder on the night of the 11th. Meanwhile, as he and three other Americans lay dying, back in the States Obama was flying out West to another high brow fundraiser so he could self-servingly get reelected.

What is most certain is that this trouble spot region was the hub of activity for special ops units comprised of special forces and a large number of CIA operatives in conjunction with British MI6. The CIA safely defended annex in Benghazi a mere mile and a half from the embassy compound was the largest CIA station in North Africa. The annex housed 35 CIA personnel responsible for coordinating the large arms smuggling operation to Syria, circumventing Congress by calling the CIA mission a liaison operation.

Two former special ops operatives Brandon Webb and Jack Murphy, authors of 'Benghazi: The Definitive Report,' have since claimed that a bureaucratic breakdown in communication between CIA and JSOC caused local Benghazi radicals to attack and kill Americans on 9/11/12. They believe that just days before an assassination carried out by Special Operations of a popular Libyan CIA informant had angered an al Qaeda affiliated militia called Ansar al-Sharia to launch the attack as retribution. The former Special Ops boys, one of whom was friends with one of the killed Americans Glen Doherty, speculated that the root cause of the American embassy deaths was the result of the left hand not knowing what the right hand was doing in the over-compartmentalized, ultra-guarded secrecy of competing clandestine intelligence operations and that this problem commonly serves as a major barrier and significant dysfunction of American foreign policy in general. They believe the Ambassador was probably only peripherally aware of the high presence of CIA and JSOC operations in the area but was never directly involved or looped in.

This claim appears to be a disinformation ploy to again absolve the higher ups Obama and Clinton of any responsibility. It did little to quiet the conjecture surrounding the attack that Stevens knew too much and had become a thorn in the side of the hierarchical status quo.

Though the former special ops authors may have offered small minor details on the Benghazi story, obviously far more was going down than they alluded to. On October 26th, 2012 a mere two weeks prior to the David Petraeus-Paula Broadwell affair broke as the scandalous headlines, Broadwell hyping her 'All In' biography of the general spoke at the University of Denver divulging her inside scoop on the Benghazi attack that had taken place a month and a half earlier. She claimed the attack on the compound was probable payback for CIA detaining local members from the same Libyan militia responsible for the assault. Or that the attackers may have been attempting to free their prisoners.

Though only one news reporter from Fox paid any attention to Paula at the time, once their tryst was exposed a short time afterwards, much speculation raised the issue that Broadwell unwittingly revealed classified information that could well have been leaked through her intimacy with the then CIA Director. That the mistress was privy to such insider lowdown compromising sensitive US intelligence operations headquartered at the CIA Benghazi annex is a very real possibility, especially since classified documents were later uncovered at her North Carolina home.

In view of the CIA's fervent denial that any prisoners were detained in Benghazi and Obama's January 2009 executive order outlawing the CIA business of holding prisoners,

Paula shooting her mouth off as an insider know-it-all implicated her lover Petraeus and his CIA as criminals engaging in an unlawful operation. But then that illegal activity amounts to small peanuts in comparison to the much bigger crime being committed by her lover CIA boss Petraeus and his crime bosses Obama and Hillary for using the same Libyan al Qaeda militants who murdered the four Americans on 9/11/12 to smuggle guns from Benghazi across international borders to be used against Assad in Syria.

Despite Ambassador Stevens' repeated requests for more security, it was never given. So when about 150 members of the local militia Ansar al-Sharia stormed the gates of the compound carrying machine guns and rocket propelled grenades (RPG's), the handful of unarmed Libyan security contractors instantly fled and soon enough the building was engulfed in flames.

The nearby annex in Benghazi where thirty-five CIA operatives worked was called during the crisis to assist those Americans at the embassy. CIA security officer Tyrone Woods convinced his supervisor at the annex with five other security personnel to rush to the embassy's aid. Both Woods and Glen Doherty were former Navy Seals commandos who died from bullet wounds at the second attack at the annex killed by a mortar after Sean Smith, an information officer, and Ambassador Stevens had already died from smoke inhalation.

According to authors Webb and Murphy, due to Woods and Doherty's heroics along with four other CIA analysts, the remaining embassy staff were apparently able to safely escape the burning compound. An overhead surveillance drone had been dispatched above the compound prior to that second attack that occurred at the annex.

President Obama, Secretary of State Clinton and CIA Director Petraeus were all informed of the crisis unfolding during the afternoon local Washington time. Yet they chose to not even bother contacting the Marines stationed in the capital Tripoli, allegedly figuring they would take too long to arrive on the scene in Benghazi. So after ignoring the Ambassador's pleas urging for more security for three straight months, they coldly refused to order any further military assistance at the time the four Americans lost their lives.

Instead they ordered UN Ambassador Susan Rice to later lie to the American public claiming that the attack was instigated by that anti-Moslem youtube video. Under the increasing pressure of Benghazi questions, suddenly Hillary keeled over with a brain clot to conveniently dodge any more heat. And of course Petraeus was soon engulfed in scandal with his mistress Broadwell, retiring from the CIA and out of sight for months thereafter, conveniently ducking from his hot seat. And then soon enough Clinton was resigning as Secretary of State, evading any further scrutiny as the Ambassador's boss most responsible for the deaths of the four Americans.

Another piece of incriminating evidence is that the FBI team sent in to investigate the Benghazi murders never even arrived at the crime scene until three weeks after the attack, making sure that vital forensic evidence could be conveniently lost, confiscated or destroyed. Despite having videotape that allowed individual attackers to be identified by name, they all still remain free to this day. Eleven months after the attack the US Justice

Department last August in a hollow gesture officially charged the alleged suspects in a sealed indictment. But without them in custody, it means nothing.

Clinton strategically figured she would lay low long enough out of the public spotlight to effectively distance herself from Benghazi to make another run for President in 2016. But while briefly still back on the job and those nagging Benghazi questions weren't going away fast enough, she completely lost it, screaming, "What difference at this point does it make?" – obviously all the difference in the world to her and her buddy Barrack. On 9/11 the year before last, Obama, Clinton and Petraeus sacrificed four American lives that day to preserve their own careers as powerful evil despots who with blind ambition would stop at nothing to remain in power.

President Obama and Hillary Clinton have both gone to great lengths to make sure that their cover-up concealing the truth never gets exposed. With the attack taking place less than two months prior to Obama's reelection, they are determined that the truth never sees the light of day. However, big cracks are looming in their wall of defense and their lies are falling like a house of cards. Mounting evidence indicates both Obama and Clinton were engaged in a highly covert and illicit arms smuggling operation moving weapons from Libya through Turkey to the anti-Assad rebels in Syria. And at stake for Obama and Clinton was their future plans to win the presidential election in 2012 and 2016.

On August 2nd, 2013 three full weeks prior to the sarin gas attack in the Damascus suburb killing scores of Syrian civilians including children, UK'sTelegraph reporter Damien McElroy wrote an article asserting that Obama and Hillary are guilty as charged, engaging in a gun-running operation that included surface to air missiles and even chemical weapons speculating that a "false flag operation" might occur as a deceptive ploy to make false accusations against Assad. Again, this article came out three weeks PRIOR to Obama accusing Assad of using chemical weapons. No coincidence in the timing. Since then renowned investigative reporter Seymour Hersh who broke the My Lai massacre story and cover-up during the Vietnam War and a host of other journalists have since provided convincing evidence that the chemical attack last August was committed by US backed al Qaeda rebels.

And those 35 CIA agents stationed at the nearby Benghazi annex, word came out that every month since the event they have been required to undergo polygraph tests just to ensure they keep quiet. One insider even told **CNN** last year, "You jeopardize your family as well if you talk to anyone about what happened."

Aside from Obama, Hillary and Petraeus evading accountability at all cost, what is most incriminating is that the very same Al Qaeda jihadists armed, financed and supported with American taxpayer dollars during the Libyan regime-change are the exact same individuals who have gotten away with murdering those four Americans in Benghazi. For more than three years now America and Saudi Arabia have been sponsoring and funding al Qaeda affiliated militia groups from all over the Middle East and North Africa fighting Assad forces in Syria in the latest regime-change war.

When the murders went down on 9/11/12, Hillary's State Department had been acting as a cover supporting al Qaeda elements smuggling arms to Syria to fight in that so called civil war. Much of Gaddafi's huge stash of arms had been looted, falling into the hands of American-backed rebel forces in Libya, including chemical weapons that were never accounted for. By pure accident, the Benghazi tragedy reveals the ongoing war by proxy that the US, Saudi Arabia and Israel have been waging against Syria and its strongest allies Iran and Russia.

As a side note, ex-CIA Director Petraeus was allowed to retain his full status as a retired four star general at full pay despite committing adultery while still serving as Afghanistan War commander when military personnel of lower rank are customarily demoted and forced to retire at a lower pension rate for the exact same offense of adultery. Mistress Paula Broadwell also suffered no formal consequence regarding her retention rank as major in the US Army Reserves. It seems obvious that Petraeus has been rewarded for his loyal silence on the Benghazi incident. Additionally, several days after Petraeus ducked out of sight in disgrace after resigning as CIA Director, Petraeus' wife as the victim of his adulterous affair was suddenly being promoted by Obama to a new cushy position made especially for her earning near Petraeus' retirement pension of $200,000 per year.

Then just over a week after his CIA resignation Petraeus was called in to testify before the House Intelligence Committee but given a free pass in his not having to testify under a sworn oath to disclose the full truth of what he knew. So he proceeded to lie before Congress claiming that he consistently said that an al Qaeda affiliated militia group was behind the attack. In fact Petraeus secretly flew to Libya immediately after the attack and upon his return to the US a couple days later Petraeus held the official administration line they knew to be false that the Benghazi attack was due to the bogus anti-Moslem video.

Of course with the scandal causing his own presidential ambitions to be thoroughly shattered, Petraeus more recently has gone on public record stating that Hillary Clinton would make "an excellent president." Clearly he is towing the line as a good little boy for keeping his mouth shut for Hillary and Barrack.
Obama lied when he promised to ensure that those guilty of the attack would be brought to justice. Now going on two years later not one of the attackers has even been apprehended or arrested.

With the murderers in the Benghazi assault still at large, many of the attackers afterwards moved on with the arms they were helping to smuggle to join US-supported rebel forces fighting the Assad government in Syria. They may have been silenced by now, secretly killed by judge, jury and executioner President Obama in his lust to kill his enemies with drone missile attacks. In any event, rest assure none of the perpetrators behind the Benghazi attack will ever be captured alive or prosecuted. They simply know too much. Last 9/11/13 barely a peep was heard from the mainstream media on the very first anniversary of the Benghazi tragedy. The reason is all too obvious.

Many of the family members of the murdered Americans felt that Obama and his administration were responsible for their loved ones deaths. Some complained about Obama's condolences as brusk, insincere and insensitive. They were disturbed further with

Obama's response on a 60 Minutes segment in late January 2013. Obama and Hillary were answering questions about Benghazi when Obama quoted Defense Secretary Robert Gates, "At this moment somewhere, somehow, somebody in the federal government's screwing up" as he turned to Hillary laughing at his joke about their Benghazi screw-up that killed four Americans. They also had to be upset hearing the president on another occasion callously dismissing the Benghazi tragedy as "a sideshow."

Not surprisingly, the US installed puppet government in Libya has been of no assistance in its lack of cooperation with revealing any further details of the attack. Last June the chaos, lawlessness and terror in Benghazi only continued as thirty-one Libyans protesting their grievances against an al Qaeda militia group were brutally massacred outside the al Qaeda headquarters. The entire eastern region of Libya today is still not under control of the national government, which has largely been taken over by US backed al Qaeda affiliates. Libya today is in complete shambles steeped in corruption, instability and violence.

Meanwhile, the two American criminals most responsible for the attack, President Obama and presidential heir-apparent Hilary Clinton need to be held accountable for their crimes along with their other partner-in-crime General Petraeus. With the belated truth behind Benghazi slowly coming out, Obama should be impeached and Hillary must never become president. Ironically the crime of Nixon's Watergate cover-up that brought down the first and only president in US history forced to resign in disgrace pales in comparison to the crimes committed by the likes of the Obama administration

Interventionists

Robert Kagan describes as his "mainstream" view of American force is his relationship with former Secretary of State Hillary Rodham Clinton, who remains the vessel into which many interventionists are pouring their hopes.

Mr. Kagan pointed out that he had recently attended a dinner of foreign-policy experts at which Mrs. Clinton was the guest of honor, and that he had served on her bipartisan group of foreign-policy heavy hitters at the State Department, where his wife worked as her spokeswoman.

"I feel comfortable with her on foreign policy," Mr. Kagan said, adding that the next step after Mr. Obama's more realist approach "could theoretically be whatever Hillary brings to the table" if elected president. "If she pursues a policy which we think she will pursue," he added, "it's something that might have been called neocon, but clearly her supporters are not going to call it that; they are going to call it something else."

After nearly a decade in the political wilderness, the neoconservative movement is back. . . . Even as they castigate Mr. Obama, the neocons may be preparing a more brazen feat: aligning themselves with Hillary Rodham Clinton and her nascent presidential campaign, in a bid to return to the driver's seat of American foreign policy. . . .

Other neocons have followed Kagan's careful centrism and respect for Mrs. Clinton. Max Boot, a senior fellow at the Council on Foreign Relations, noted in The New Republic this year that "it is clear that in administration councils she was a principled voice for a strong stand on controversial issues, whether supporting the Afghan surge or the intervention in Libya."

And the thing is, these neocons have a point. Mrs. Clinton voted for the Iraq war; supported sending arms to Syrian rebels; likened Russia's president, Vladimir V. Putin, to Adolf Hitler; wholeheartedly backs Israel; and stresses the importance of promoting democracy.

It's easy to imagine Mrs. Clinton's making room for the neocons in her administration. No one could charge her with being weak on national security with the likes of Robert Kagan on board. . . . Far from ending, then, the neocon odyssey is about to continue. In 1972, Robert L. Bartley, the editorial page editor of The Wall Street Journal and a man who championed the early neocon stalwarts, shrewdly diagnosed the movement as representing "something of a swing group between the two major parties." Despite the partisan battles of the early 2000s, it is remarkable how very little has changed.

So take that, cynics. There are pockets of vibrant political excitement stirring in the land over a Hillary Clinton presidency. There are posters being made, buttons being appended, checks being prepared, appointments being coveted. The joint, allied, synergistic constituencies of plutocracy and endless war have their beloved candidate. And it's really quite difficult to argue that their excitement and affection are unwarranted.

The Israel Lobby

Should she become president, on one level, better ties with Israel are virtually guaranteed. Let's not forget that the Clintons dealt with Bibi too as prime minister. It was never easy. But clearly it was a lot more productive than what we see now.

To put it simply, as a more conventional politician, Hillary is good on Israel and relates to the country in a way Obama doesn't. Hillary is from a different generation and functioned in a political world in which being good on Israel was both mandatory and smart.

When it comes to Israel, there is no Bill Clinton 2.0. The former president is probably unique among presidents for the depth of his feeling for Israel and his willingness to put aside his own frustrations with certain aspects of Israel's behavior, such as settlements. But this accommodation applies to Hillary too. Both Bill and Hillary are so enamored with the idea of Israel and its unique history that they are prone to make certain allowances for the reality of Israel's behavior, such as the continuing construction of settlements.

Netanyahu

Have you been wondering why Hillary Clinton has been so silent as the Obama administration and newly-reelected Prime Minister Benjamin Netanyahu have been at each others throats? Presumably, a presidential candidate leading every other Democratic challenger for the nomination would have something to say on such a monumental U.S. foreign policy issue. The subject is Israel for god's sake, not the island nation of Guam!

Well, now we know. In a late-night statement, Malcolm Hoenlein -- the Executive Vice Chairman of the Conference of Presidents of Major American Jewish Organizations -- told media organizations what Secretary Clinton supposedly thinks of the Barack-Bibi spat. The statement was as general and vague as words can be, but if you're a member of Joe-public like I am, it at least provides you with some sense of what Clinton is thinking.

"Secretary Clinton thinks we need to all work together to return the special U.S.-Israel relationship to constructive footing, to get back to basic shared concerns and interests, including a two-state solution pursued through direct negotiations between Israelis and Palestinians," Mr. Hoenlein said. "We must ensure that Israel never becomes a partisan issue."

This is about as safe a remark Hillary Clinton could have given. What prospective 2016 presidential candidate doesn't want to improve the U.S.-Israel relationship? It's about as obvious as saying that the government should fight animal abuse. And what presidential candidate doesn't support a two-state solution to the Israeli-Palestinian conflict?

Democratic and Republican presidents over a period of decades have argued that negotiating two states for two peoples is the only viable way to solve this intractable conflict. After all, there isn't a better alternative: Israeli annexation of the West Bank, a one-state solution, a three-state solution, or temporary, interim Palestinian governance over select portions of the West Bank and Gaza aren't exactly recipes for long-term stability.

But beneath the obvious, read between the lines and you come to an equally obvious conclusion: Clinton believes that the Obama administration is mismanaging relations with Benjamin Netanyahu, a man that has proven to be an incredibly difficult person to deal with (James Baker and Bill Clinton can attest to this) on issues as important as preventing Iran from attaining a nuclear weapon and establishing a democratic and demilitarized Palestinian state alongside Israel. Politically speaking, Hillary Clinton is trying her best to distance herself from an administration whose second-term foreign policy approval ratings are awful and a White House that staunch pro-Israel supporters in Congress and across the country are convinced has an interest in continuing the diplomatic crisis. Or as Abe Foxman, President of the Anti-Defamation League, said to *The Jerusalem Post*, "I am...troubled by statements now coming out of the White House."

It would be easy to chock up Hillary's maneuver as politics during the beginning of her presidential campaign and call it day. But there's something more to it than that: relations between a U.S. President and an Israeli Prime Minister are the worst they have been since the early 1990s. Bibi Netanyahu has a lot to do with this downward spiral, including his comments on Election Day about Arab Israelis streaming to the polls "in droves" and his remark about a Palestinian state being an impossibility during his tenure. But, to his credit, Bibi seems to have recognized that his comments were ill-conceived and counterproductive, and has gone as far as apologizing for being insensitive to the concerns of Israel's Arab citizens. For a man like Netanyahu, apologizing publicly is a big deal.

The White House, however, is unfazed by Netanyahu and has consistently expressed reservations about the Israeli Prime Minister's judgment and sincerity. From White House Press Secretary Josh Earnest and State Department Spokeswoman Jen Psaki to President Obama himself, Netanyahu is molded as an insincere politician who will do anything to save his job -- even if it means foreclosing a two-state solution that he previously supported and which Middle East experts, the U.S. and Israeli governments, and the Arab League have all acknowledged is the only way to assure that Israel is secure and the Palestinians are recognized as full members of the international community. One can perhaps understand the administration's reluctance to accept Netanyahu's about-face, but the White House isn't making matters easier by questioning the prime minister in public.

Hillary Clinton has a complicated relationship with Netanyahu herself. The two have gotten into shouting matches before when the former was Secretary of State (see this article from the *Washington Post's* Anne Gearon for context), most notably over Israeli settlements on land that the Palestinians consider part of any territory that they would be allowed to keep. But, by Hillary's own admission (see her memoir, *Hard Choices*), she was able to work with Netanyahu and stroke his ego when she needed to.

Until she is able to win a presidential election, we won't know for sure whether a President Hillary Clinton would have used the same tactics with Netanyahu as President Obama has for the past six years. But, based on her record as first lady, Senator from New York, and Secretary of State, one could come to the conclusion that she wouldn't have let her personal feelings with a world leader gather so much momentum that the state-to-state relationship itself was questioned.

Hillary Clinton sees an opening that she can exploit. If elected president, one of her first orders of business would be to turn a page on U.S.-Israel relations to a more "constructive footing." But first, she needs to win that election.

Israel's election Tuesday could have an outsize impact on U.S. politics, but for Hillary Clinton, it's difficult to know what outcome she might prefer.

But while she speaks highly of him, it's not in the warmest of tones. "I've known Bibi a long time and I have a very good relationship with him, in part because we can yell at each other, and we do," she told CNN last year, using to a nickname for the prime minister. "And I was often the designated yeller."

In her 2014 memoir "Hard Choices," in which Clinton tends to portray others in the most flattering light possible, her description of Netanyahu as a "complicated figure" is decidedly more muted.

She had, by contrast a "close friendship" with Yitzhak Rabin, the former Israeli prime minister who was assassinated by a radical right-wing Israeli during Bill Clinton's first term in the White House.

After a short stint by Rabin's successor, Shimon Peres, Netanyahu took over the prime ministership in 1996 and served for most of the remainder of Clinton's term. Netanyahu "believes [he] lost him the prime ministership" in 1999, as Hillary Clinton said last year in an interview, because he signed a peace deal struck with Bill Clinton that included giving land to the Palestinians.

In 1998, Netanyahu and his wife took the Clintons to visit the Masada, a mountainous fort and one of the country's major landmarks, just days before Clinton would be impeached back in Washington.

More recently, Israel's 2009 election was one of Clinton's first tests as secretary of state. The Kadima Party and it's leader, TzipiLivni, actually won more seats, but failed to form a government, and Netanyahu was able to retake his old job.
In her book, Clinton wrote that she called Livni to suggest she join a coalition government with Netanyahu's Likud party, which Clinton thought might have a better chance of striking a peace deal with the Palestinians than a government by Netanyahu. But Livni declined to share power with Netanyahu.
Valerie Jarrett on Clinton emails

This year, longtime Clinton message guru Paul Begala went to Israel to help Netanyahu's rival, and several strategists who worked for Barack Obama and could potentially join a Clinton campaign – led by field organizer Jeremy Bird – are working with a nonprofit that opposes Netanyahu. Clinton's longtime pollster, Stan Greenberg, has worked for the opposition Labor Party in the past as well.

Netanyahu has grown increasingly conservative in the lead-up to Tuesday's tight election, saying this week that there will be no Palestinian state if he wins.

In a field in Iowa last summer, Bill Clinton gave perhaps his most candid thoughts on Netanyahu when a C-SPAN microphone caught him agreeing that Netanyahu is "not the guy" to bring peace to the region.

An American neoconservative group backing Netanyahu ran a commercial last month attacking Clinton for not speaking out against Democratic lawmakers' plans to boycott Netanyahu's recent speech to Congress. "Does she support the boycotters? Or is she too afraid to stand up to them?" the ad asked.

Clinton did not meet with Netanyahu while he was in town, though they were both in Washington on the same day.

Presumptive Democratic presidential candidate Hillary Clinton weighed in on America's policy toward Israel in the aftermath of the re-election of Prime Minister Benjamin Netanyahu on Sunday, telling a group of Jewish leaders that the United States must work with all sides of the conflict in support of a two-state solution to the Israel-Palestinian conflict.

The comments, which were first reported by the New York Times, appear to differ from President Barack Obama's pledge to re-evaluate the United States' policy toward Israel in the aftermath of Netanyahu's election-eve claim that he would not work toward the establishment of a Palestinian state during his fourth term as prime minister. They also come as relations between Obama and Netanyahu have deteriorated over disagreements about America's ongoing negotiations to contain Iran's nuclear program, Israel's continued expansion of settlements in the occupied territories, and other issues.

"[W]hat we can't do is pretend that there's a possibility of something that's not there," Obama said in response to a question about the probability of pursuing a two-state solution through direct negotiations between Netanyahu and the Palestinians, adding, "we can't continue to premise our public diplomacy based on something that everybody knows is not going to happen at least in the next several years." Obama's administration has condemned Netanyahu's remarks and floated the possibility of pursuing peace through multi-national organizations like the United Nations, despite the prime minister's efforts to walk back his comments.

But in her newly publicized statements, Clinton appeared to have held her fire against Netanyahu and suggested that she believes she could attain a two-state solution through the bilateral track — a longstanding practice of American policy and one that Clinton herself worked on as Secretary of State.

In fact, as recently as 2014, Clinton seemed to believe that Netanyahu is truly interested in eventually creating an independent Palestinian state alongside Israel, something Obama and most Arab leaders have rejected.

"I really believe that if [Netanyahu] thought he could get adequate security guarantees for a long enough period of time, he would be able to resolve everything with the exception of Jerusalem which is the hardest issue," Clintontold CNN's Fareed Zakaria in July of 2014. In that interview, she described her relationship with Netanyahu as "very good" and profoundly honest. "[W]e can yell at each other, and we do. And I was often the designated yeller. Something would happen, a new settlement announcement would come and I would call him up, what are you doing? You've got to stop this," she said.

Mara Rudman, a deputy envoy and chief of staff for the Office of the Special Envoy for Middle East Peace at the State Department from 2009 to 2011, confirmed that Clinton herself was "quite intensely involved" in the Obama administration's effort to restart the peace process and worked closely with former Sen. George Mitchell, who served as Obama's envoy to the region during that period. She too described Clinton's relationship with the Israeli prime minister as "good."

Still, Rudman stressed that any new president will have to re-assess the state of America's relationship with its international allies and pursue a policy that she or he believes is in the best national security interest of the United States.

"You figure out what you need to do for your country to play out United States interests and in some cases that's going to involve needing to repair relationships, in some cases that's going to involve building new relationships, in some cases that's going to involve just picking up where the last administration, Democrat or Republican, may have left off. It will be a variety of things," Rudman — who has also served on several presidential transition teams — said during a phone interview with ThinkProgress.

As for Obama's very public rebuke of Netanyahu, which Clinton has not echoed, Rudman wondered if his strategy does more harm than good to bringing peace to the region. "What I wonder about is what benefit you get from raising the volume high on a public stage and whether that increases your options when you're the United States or whether it ends up decreasing your options," she said, adding "I continue to believe there is a route for private diplomacy." It appearsthat Clinton agrees.